Get Rich with Digital Real Estate

"Quitters Never Win and Winners Never Quit"

Chapters

Foreword - Seven Income Streams

A well-known maxim is that the average millionaire has seven income streams, often in diverse channels. Having multiple income streams in diverse channels is powerful because of the ebbs and flows of any business. If one channel underperforms one month, it's likely that the other channels will overperform providing balance and sustained revenue. Traditionally, creating income streams in separate channels was difficult to accomplish. Creating diverse income channels used to require a lot of capital. Today, we have the internet. There are now many opportunities to create income streams that require little to no capital, often just sweat equity.

Everyone knows that there are a lot of different ways to make money in internet marketing. What a lot of people don't tell you is that you should do as many of them as you can. Consider this - one of my favorite statistics is that the average person reads two books a year. In reality, the average person reads zero books a year. Where does that two book average come from then? The answer is that people who do read, read so many books, that it skews the average up. How many income streams do you think the average millionaire actually has?

The ability to fast forward to the revenue security that millionaires have, even before becoming a millionaire, has never been easier. In my ten years in internet marketing I have created an SEO agency, High Voltage SEO, a SAAS tool, PageOptimizer Pro, an online community, Internet Marketing Gold, and several revenue generating websites. All of those ventures required very little capital and are now generating high levels of revenue. Additionally, if one source has a down month, the other sources pick up the slack.

Creating income streams doesn't happen overnight, but there are shortcuts. You can learn from the best to give yourself the best chance at success. Rank and

4

Rent, as taught by Mike, is one of the methods you should consider adding to your income streams. Read this book, implement the strategies, and take one step closer to financial security and becoming a modern millionaire.

Kyle Roof

Introduction

A man noticed no cages or chains were used to hold the elephants during a stroll through an elephant sanctuary.

A small piece of rope tied to one of their legs was the only thing preventing them from escaping the camp.

Observing the elephants, he was utterly baffled as to why the elephants didn't simply use their strength to break the rope and escape the camp. Even though they could have done so easily, they did not.

Inquiring as to why the elephants stood there instead of attempting escape, the young man asked a nearby trainer.

He replied;

"When they are very young, we tie them with the same size rope, and at that age, it is enough to hold them. As the Elephants grow up, they are taught to believe that they cannot break away. Consequently, they never try to break away from the rope because they believe it will hold them."

Only because they adopted the belief that it couldn't be done over the years that the elephants don't break free and escape from the camp.

They could simply start walking, and the rope would snap without effort.

Keep believing that what you want to accomplish is possible no matter how much the world tries to hold you back. To achieve success, you need to believe it can be done.

Many people still believe that online businesses are not real, and therefore they never try. They are as real and as profitable as any business. You will see inside this book.

The world of property rentals has always been a very profitable one. Landlords who rent out on a large scale have been one of the most well-paid people of the past 200 years. However, this industry has always been reserved for the already rich. The Internet has changed this and has enabled something called Rank & Rent. This means you can actually build your own online digital assets and rent them out for a high monthly fee. You become a digital Landlord, and it is just as profitable as being a real-world property owner, but with almost none of the initial outlay.

There isn't much difference between a property landlord and a digital property landlord or Rank & Rent expert. They both rent out their assets for a profit and make a significant income. The more property they can acquire, the more money they make.

Let me give you an example.

Brian invests $200,000 into a property, he spends $20,000 on getting it ready to be rented out, then he takes it to a realtor, and they rent it out for him. He makes $1,000 a month for this property, less the mortgage and the realtors fees. He has $220,000 invested, and he will earn $1,000 a month less expenses.

James invests $100 on building a website, then spends another $200 on ranking it on the first page of Google. He advertises his website in a Facebook group for Rank & Rent. He rents it out for $1,000 a month with almost no overheads whatsoever.

Brian has $220,000 invested to generate $1,000 a month, and James only $300 invested, but they make the same income.

Which industry seems more profitable to you?

Now imagine you reinvest the first $1000 you make into more websites. They cost you $100 each to build and $200 each to rank. That's 3 more digital assets you have to rent out at $1000 each per month. Even if you spend every penny you make from this point forward, after a few months, you are making $4000 a month and have 4 websites, and this is nearly all profit. Do this part-time for an entire year, don't spend all the money, but instead reinvest it into new sites and be strict with what you do. There is no reason you can't have a 7 figure a year repeat income business within the next 12 months.

When you are working in Rank & Rent, the very first thing to do is start with the end in mind. What I mean by this is you build a business that one day won't need you. Suppose you build a business that one day will not require you to run it, that can still pay you a hefty monthly wage. You've created an appreciating asset that provides not only income but a lifestyle where you no longer need to work. Once you have enough money, it's not more money you want. It's more freedom, so let's make a mental note of this right now.

First, we work to make money, then we work for freedom.

With this in mind, we focus on finding software that can automate as much as possible. We focus on simplicity so that anybody can take over our role with very little skill. Anything that can be automated is automated. Which will reduce costs for our business and save us using the one thing we can get any more of, our time.

I will teach you exactly how to do this and precisely what software you need to use inside this book.

Where To Get Started

Gold-seeking miners were forced to quit their jobs during the gold rush because they had not yet struck gold and had begun to tire. Other men continued mining where they left off. The new miners went just three feet and struck gold. The first miners were just three feet from success and a rich life, but they instead chose failure.

Stay strong in the face of adversity. Many people give up on following their dreams because the work becomes too difficult, tedious, or tiresome-but sometimes you're closer to the finish line than you think. If you work just a little harder, you will succeed.

When I first discovered the Rank & Rent business model, I thought I would take over the world. I decided I was going to Build, Rank & Rent out websites in hundreds of industries. I was like, I'm going to take this industry. So, I started with five Plumbers, Roofers, Electricians, Locksmiths and Pest Control.

I wanted to target all these industries myself and completely crush them. So, I set out on my journey of world domination. I really did feel like I could take the world. I started building websites in all five industries. I was researching all five industries. I was writing content in all five industries. I was building backlinks in all five industries. And before I knew it, I became a busy fool.

My days were filled with busy, my head was filled with clutter, but my bank wasn't filled with money.

Had I given up at this point, I would have quit just 3 feet from success.

I discussed my dilemma with my mother, who was still alive at the time, and she just smiled at me because she knows what I'm like. I'm always trying to take over the world.

She just said, "One step at a time, Michael." Confused, I asked what she meant.

Then she asked me a question.

"What happens if we focus on too many things at once?"

"I don't know," I was still actually confused.

"You can't give anything your full attention. So, nothing gets done right. Pick an industry and take that first."

Now, I'd heard this so many times before about focus. People say multitasking destroys productivity and focus, making it really difficult for you to do anything right. But I never realized that I was multitasking until my mother actually pointed it out and said, this is what you're doing. She was right. I was jumping from one thing to another. Never giving anything my full attention. Does this happen to you? You keep jumping from one great idea to another great idea to another great idea but never actually get anything done?

On this occasion, I listened to my mother for the first time in my life, and I decided to take locksmiths. All my effort went into building locksmith websites. All my studying was based around locksmiths and their websites. I looked at terminology. I looked at how people searched online for locksmiths. I even looked at how many backlinks were built on average to general locksmith websites. Within a few months, I had dozens of websites built and ranking. Some were rented out, and some I actually sold the leads directly to local businesses on a lead-by-lead basis. I became well known in the industry as a specialist for locksmith websites. Within 12 months, I had over 200 businesses renting my websites or paying me for leads every month.

So let me ask you, from what we've just gone through. What is the number one rule you must follow when building your own Rank & Rent business?

The number one rule you must follow when starting out is choosing a niche and sticking with it.

I want you to find a profitable niche and stick with it until you're known as a specialist in that niche.

Why do you want to become a specialist rather than just moving from niche to niche?

A specialist can charge more money. All your research pays off and helps for every website you build. Your content writing is easier, faster and more effective. Everything you do as a specialist is more effective because you can spend time on that niche. You're not all over the place. You benefit from all the work you've done repeatedly. You're able to focus on what you're doing rather than being pulled in multiple directions.

So, choose a niche and become a specialist in that niche.

How To Find a Profitable Niche

Stefan from Bulgaria was released from prison and wanted to build his own business but did not know where to start. My company was much smaller at the time, and he contacted me directly to ask if my strategy could work for him. I explained he didn't need an education or to be the most intelligent guy in the room to follow the process. However, he should follow the strategy to the letter and spend at least a couple of hours a day on building his new business.

He purchased Magic Page Plugin about 3 years ago, followed the strategy and targeted an emergency services niche which, unfortunately, I've sworn not to divulge.

After just 6 months, Stefan had more than 30 websites ranking on Google generating him over $18,000 every single month.

I touch base with Stefan regularly, even though he has refused to give me a testimonial to this day. Why? Because he is petrified that someone will get onto his niche. Stefan no longer works as hard as initially but has still managed to triple his monthly income over the last few years.

He is one of my favorite success stories, and I feel proud that what I managed to teach him has enabled him to have a wonderful life and remain out of prison. I may take credit for teaching him this and be super proud of what he has done. Still, he took the teaching, implemented it and secured himself a much better future.

At the other end of the scale and unfortunately on a much more regular basis. I have clients come to me with ideas that just will not work, and I'm entirely open and honest with them about this.

As entrepreneurs, we do not listen and drive forward with our idea even though it does not fit into this business model and will not work on a large scale.

When you decide to do Rank & Rent, you need to take a few things into account before starting.

There are a few minor elements that will make an enormous difference to a business. The number one is that you must target an industry that is going to be profitable.

Let me share a few key things that you should consider when doing this that will seem obvious. However, most people forget to do them when starting a business.

The first and maybe most important is commercial intent. Your website has to have some sort of commercial intent. If it doesn't, no business will pay for the traffic it generates. The likelihood of you ever being able to rent it out is almost nil.

You might be at the top of Google. You may have the number one position in every single area in the entire country. But if nobody can make money from it, nobody's going to pay you for it.

Commercial intent is one of the most important things to consider when first setting up.

Also, you either want something that has high search volume in Google or is high value. If you can find something with high search volume and high value, you've hit the jackpot. This industry will obviously make you a heck of a lot of money once you rank in it.

So, in a perfect world. We would have commercial intent with high search volume and high-value keywords. However, you may not get all three. If you can get high search volume with commercial intent or high value with commercial intent, you're starting in the right place.

Pick A Niche That Will Work

Okay, so you've found an industry that you want to go after. You now know that it has plenty of searches or high-value keywords, and there is commercial intent.

Once you have chosen a potential industry, you are happy to say that this is the industry you want to pursue. Before you rush to move forward and possibly waste your time, there are a few more things you should consider.

First - Do they want more business?

This might seem obvious, and you might think that all companies want more business, but this isn't always the case.

I used to work for an engineering firm, and they sold very high-value industrial ovens that they used to manufacture. When I left that company, I wondered if I could get into that industry myself. When I looked at it, there were five firms in the entire country. They kept the prices high, hardly used Google ads, and wouldn't pay any third-party companies at all ever for business, and they were booked up 12 months in advance. On the face of it, a lead is worth £500 to £1000, but no one will pay for it, so really, it's worth zero.

So, when considering this, find out if there are companies in that industry who actually want more business or need more business. Are they booked out entirely for the next two or three years? If so, there's no point in starting working in this industry because you will never rent out your website. In this type of industry, a customer will actually have to chase the company, not the other way round.

You should also consider. Can businesses in the industry afford to pay for the website? For example, if you're going after somebody who does dog walking. I can't imagine that they generate hundreds of thousands or millions every single year.

They can't afford to pay a high value for their websites each month or even pay at all. Most of the work that comes into them is likely from word of mouth.

On the other hand, if you were going after locksmiths or plumbers, you know they have higher than average earnings. They also generate a lot of money from every job they do and can afford to pay for their websites.

Now Choose a Sub-Niche

You're probably looking at this, swearing saying, "what the F*** is Mike making me do this for? He just told me to find an industry, and now he's saying choose a sub-niche." What does he want me to do?

Well, you have chosen an industry that will work for you. However, to do this and be able to dominate a specific section of a market, what you now need to do is choose a sub-niche. So, for example, let's say you decided on Plumbing. That's a great industry, but don't go after plumbers in general because it is too big and too hard and will take you months to see decent results on your websites.

Instead, go after boiler repairs, or go after boiler installations, or go after leaking pipes. I'm saying this because I want you to create an entire website that's kind of like Wikipedia or an Encyclopedia of a specific section or sub-niche of the industry.

You will find these types of websites rank a lot faster. You get a lot more work in. When speaking to potential website renters in the industry, you can get them to rent your site a lot easier. If you say to a renter, you will only receive jobs for boiler repairs from this website. Or you're only going to receive leak repairs, or you're only going to get boiler installations. They are much more likely to buy because it's their target work.

They know what type of work they're getting, can then look at it and say right if a boiler installation makes me $3,000. I'm paying $1000 a month for this site, I only need one job a month from this website, and I've tripled my money.

Realistically, they might get two jobs, or three, or five, or even 10 Jobs a month, and they will never leave. It will also make it easier for you to justify the site's value because you know what leads it provides.

Those who know me and have followed me for a long time online will know that one of my favorite sayings is inch-wide mile-deep. Now what I mean by that is, find a subsection of the broader industry that is very narrow. It's specific but has a lot of work in it, precisely like boiler repair, or underfloor heating, or boiler installation and go after that.

When I say mile deep, what I mean by that is there's a hell of a lot of work in the inch-wide subsection, and we're going to specialize in that.

Instead of saying we only target Manchester, you target this sub-niche in many locations and rent your websites to multiple businesses.

This means you have more people getting the calls or receiving information from the website or network of websites. Leadsimplify.com will assist you in segregating calls and separating leads if you want to automate this.

So, you're looking to go after an inch wide mile deep section of a specific industry with commercial intent and high searches, high value or both.

The first step is to choose your sub-niche. Next, you pursue that sub-niche. Once you have become a specialist in that area, you can build all of your websites around it.

Once you've chosen a sub-niche, start building a fantastic website in that sub-niche. What you then want to be doing is target a specific location with a view to spreading across the country city by city as you grow. We call it spreading like a wave, and the reason we spread like a wave is straightforward. Word of mouth will sell the new sites for you. If you've got a plumber that covers Manchester, he might also cover Liverpool and will take both websites off you. If he doesn't, then there's a good chance he knows somebody in Liverpool that will take your website off you.

A great way to get somebody to pass your sites on by word of mouth is simply by turning around and saying, I'll give you 10% of everything they spend with me. They will even help when you have issues with that buyer in the future because you are paying them.

Let's say you bring in $1000 a month, and you give them $100 a month. They will also be keen to rent out all of your other websites in all the other major cities everywhere in the country. A plumber will rent a website from another plumber long before they rent a website from you. A recommendation is the best form of marketing. It makes it a lot easier to rent out your websites than it would be if you contacted the businesses directly.

You find your first plumber, and they become your top sales guy because they know every plumber in the industry and go to all the events. They also get their secret 10% on every person they get for you.

Using this strategy will really help you grow your Rank & Rent business in whatever niche you choose.

Expired Domains & Why They Help

You run your own architect business. You decide you need to take on a new member of staff. Brian, just 16 years old, has left school and is looking for a job, so you decide to give him the opportunity and take him on.

Brian works really hard for you for 5 years. You spend thousands on training him and teaching him to do the job. After 5-years, he generates some income for the business. Brian pays off in the long run, but it takes a long time and a lot of investment.

You run your own architect business. You decide to take on a new member of staff. Frank has been an architect for the last 10 years, is fully qualified, and knows what the job entails. He starts work for you on Monday, and by Friday, he's already earning the company money.

Brian is like using a new domain for your business websites, whereas Frank is like using an expired domain. Not all expired domains are created equal. Therefore, it is important to research their history just like you would a new member of staff.

Expired domains can massively reduce the time it takes a website to rank in the search engines, generate leads, traffic, and get a return on your investment.

I'm not saying you need to spend too much time studying expired domains. Still, you should always try to get a domain with some sort of history and is close to the niche you are targeting.

I like to use a free website called expireddomains.net, and I check the total number of backlinks with the total number of referring domains. If these are almost equal, I will purchase the domain and put a website on it.

I don't immediately make the website part of my network because it may be a domain that Google doesn't like. Similar to a human who has a criminal record, a domain name retains a lot of its history in Googles eyes and those that have a so called checkered past can be penalized for it. This is why I wait until Google have indexed the website before associating it with any of my other websites.

You can check if it's been indexed by typing site:yoururl.com into the Google search bar. Even though most of the time expired domains are better, we still use both expired and new domains in our networks because it looks more natural to Google.

I will talk in more detail later in the book about creating a website network that will help you rank, so do not worry about it too much at this stage. You will learn all about it in the chapter on Single Niche PBNs.

Analyzing The Competition

To analyze the competition, you must consider a few factors. The first is content, how much content they currently have on their webpage and how well the actual page is SEO optimized. Not only that, but you also need to consider the number of off-page SEO factors which help their current rankings. This includes things like social signals, traffic, bounce rate and backlinks.

A great way to figure out if a location will be challenging to rank in is by first looking at large companies like yell.com and checking if they build backlinks to that location. If you find a place where a site like Yell is ranking and hasn't created any external backlinks, you know that area is pretty easy to rank for. If companies like Yell link to the location in addition to the links they have obtained organically. They are actively pursuing rankings in that area because their content isn't sufficient to rank there.

Another great way to figure out if an area will be hard to rank is to check if any of the pages ranking on the first page of Google do not have the search term in their meta title. Suppose there are sites ranking that do not have the keyword in their meta title. In that case, this must be an easy location to rank in as the meta title is the number one ranking factor for Google.

Like with yell.com, we also want to check if there are websites on the first page of Google ranking for the keyword you're going after that do not have any backlinks pointing to them. If you can find a site on the first page of Google that does not have any backlinks, you know it is possible to win in this niche with just content alone. If you don't have any backlink checking tools, you can visit this URL and check the first 100 links any site has for free https://ahrefs.com/backlink-checker.

Find an industry where you can win with just content that has commercial intent with high value or high search volume keywords. Then long, well-written content that makes sense and is human readable and covers the subject in great detail will, in most cases, be enough to get you to the first page of Google. You will then need to consider off-page SEO once you get to the first page, and this will help move you up the rankings into the top position. We will leave off-page SEO for a little later in the book.

How SEO Experts Write Content That Ranks

Before we get started with this chapter, I want you to close the book and open a browser window on any electronic device you have access to. Go to the Google search bar and key in any keyword you want. Next, I want you to pick any website at random, or even a few of them, open them and start reading the content. I guarantee whichever website you opened has perfectly well-written content that makes sense to you, the reader. You can actually do this search for almost any keyword anywhere in the world, and the result will always be the same.

Taking this into account, it goes without saying that Google understands the content and serves up well-written quality content no matter what search the individual makes.

When I research industries and look at websites that people are creating, I notice that many websites contain completely unreadable junk content. I see a lot of so-called SEOs pushing this content as a way to build backlinks and rank your websites. Google understands content just like you, and I do. They can actually read the content and tell by reading it if a human will understand it. They know the local dialect, and they know industry-specific terms, slang and other jargon.

The key to writing top-quality SEO content is research and understanding of the industry you are writing about. If you don't know the industry you're writing about, you will write crap content that will never rank. You need to study, become an expert, and understand the industry, even if you're only creating a single website for that industry. Or you can replicate the way SEOs do it and write ranking content for any keyword in any location without being an expert.

Back in 2010, I was a full-time locksmith earning about £2500 a week. At the time, I thought that was a fortune, so I couldn't understand why I was always broke. I decided to take a deep dive into my finances and realized my overheads were more than £1700 a week. Most of this was going to SEO experts and Ad agencies.

I was sick of giving almost all my money away, so I took six weeks off work and started to study SEO day and night. By the end of the six weeks, I was confident I could do my own SEO. I got an entire crate of beer and sat and wrote down every single word I could think of relating to Locksmiths. I was a locksmith, so I knew many technical terms that a general SEO wouldn't understand. I had a considerable advantage in this niche over SEO experts.

After finishing this, I wrote a 3000-word document including every single word. I added it to my website, it skyrocketed to the top of Google.

I had found the golden ticket.

This method worked for seven years.

As you can imagine, I made a lot of money and ended up with over 200 contractors working for me nationally. Then one day, Google had an update, and overnight, all my rankings plummeted, and the phone stopped ringing.

This hit me so hard I started drinking heavily. I gained a lot of weight, became ill, and developed a horrible condition called gout, which to this day is still one of the worst pains I've ever experienced.

Things got worse from this point on, and money became a serious concern. I thought all hope was gone and started looking into other ways to promote my business. I tried Google and Bing Ads, but at an average of £15 per click, I couldn't make it profitable any longer.

I was about ready to give up altogether. When I got back in touch with a friend from school, as luck would have it, he was also an SEO expert. However, he worked for clients and had written content in hundreds of niches, all of which were still ranking strongly and generating hundreds of calls every month.

He opened up to me and shared his exact process of writing killer content that ranks in any industry. That is utterly future proof because the method changes as Google rankings change, meaning I am always in front of the crowd. I can now easily write content in any niche, even if I am not an expert.

This is the method:

- Find the keyword you want to rank for
- Find the location you want to rank the keyword for
- Change your IP address and do the search for that keyword in that location
- Go through every single web page on the first page of Google, extracting all the sections of content you think you can use.
- Then right-click, view the page source and pull in all the SEO features like meta titles, descriptions, alt tags, title tags, etc. Arrange them into SEO factors like meta, H tags keywords, and content. outbound URLs and so on
- Rewrite all the content, so it means the same, fits your needs, and passes Copyscape when done right. (Copyscape is a free plagiarism checker. The software lets you detect duplicate content and check if your text is original.)

This takes hours and sometimes days, but it results in quality content that Google loves. I changed how I did it and started doing it like this, and I have been successful with this method ever since.

It takes days to do it right, but it works every time and changes as Google does because you always work with the most relevant, up-to-date, ranking content.

This also enables you to write content on any subject, whether you're an expert or not.

This is the hardest part of Rank & Rent, and luckily for you, there is a quicker way to do this. If you go to PageReWriter.com and set up a FREE account, then submit a support ticket to support@mikemartin.zendesk.com sharing your Amazon review for this book. My team will give you 50 content credits utterly free of charge.

With this tool, you can input your keyword and pull back all the content you will ever need for that keyword. The content is broken down into all the SEO elements in seconds and then rewrites it with just a few clicks.

Honestly, this is the secret weapon to me, creating more content in a day than most SEOs can do in a month, and it's all 100% perfect every single time.

If you're happy to spend hours or days researching the content doing it the old way. Then simply follow the process above. Alternatively, you can get a free copy of the software, enabling you to write all your content much faster without researching or becoming an expert on whatever subject you are writing about.

This is my gift to you for reading my book and providing an honest testimonial.

10x The Leads You Get from Your Websites with One Piece of Content

It's 2011 Manchester, England, and I'm a full-time locksmith. This is before I was doing lead generation renting out websites, and all the crazy stuff.

I, like every locksmith in Manchester, was battling for the top of Google. The only difference between them and me is that I had the top three positions from using the technique I shared in the chapter above. Locksmith Manchester and all its variations generated over 3000 searches every single month. And I had the top three positions for all six variations.

Do you think I was happy?

Do you think I was inundated with work?

No. In fact, some days, I couldn't even fill my diary.

I was sitting in my office with my brother, figuring out how to get more work. We already had the top three positions for Manchester in Google, which is a major city and some days I would be sat twiddling my thumbs.

I was staring at a huge map of the UK that I used to have on my office wall. In fact, if you watch some of my old YouTube videos, you'll see it. I noticed Greater Manchester had hundreds of small areas. I knew locksmith Manchester and all its variations generated over 3000 searches every month but had no idea how many searches the smaller areas received.

When I started doing the research, I found almost 900 additional locations. All within 20 minutes of where I was based. I did the research, and it turned out these areas all had between 3 and 50 searches each per month for every area.

Doesn't sound like a lot, does it? Nope. Sounds pretty crap. But in total, there were over 18,000 local searches in Greater Manchester that almost nobody else was targeting. Nobody, just me.

After that day, I instantly put my brother to work building pages for every area in Greater Manchester. These pages all needed to be SEO perfect and include geolocation data, longitude and latitude, and stuff like that to rank. This was a big job, but after eight weeks of solid work and more complaining than I could take from my little brother, we finished.

Not long after this, we started to receive calls, and within a few short months, we were receiving more work than we could handle. This technique, coupled with our ability to write content that will rank in almost any location, put our company on the map.

Obviously, I wouldn't expect you to spend the next 8 weeks doing data input to make hundreds or even thousands of pages for your sites. Still, suppose you have a website, and the number of leads needs to increase. In that case, this strategy is by far the most cost-effective way to massively increase the calls and clients coming into your business or your clients business.

We have implemented a strategy across many major cities in the UK. We now generate around 15,000 calls every single month, just using this specific strategy on a single niche.

So how do we do it? Obviously, you don't want to go to Google maps, put a circle around your business, find every single location within a 30-mile, or 20-mile, or 10-mile radius of the website, and then build pages for all of them. If you want to, you can, and it will work, but that will take you weeks, and remember what we said earlier, if it can be automated, then we automate it and save time and money.

So, I'll tell you how I do it, and you can decide if you want to do it the old fashioned way or if you want to use software to completely automate the whole process.

We use a tool called Magic Page Plugin and what this tool does is enables you to go into your website, add a single page of content, set a radius. The software will build an almost SEO perfect page for every single area in that radius. You can start with 50 pages, 100 pages, 250 pages, 300 pages if you want and automatically build out from there over time.

I recommend keeping it under 200 pages. Otherwise, you may struggle to index the web pages. You can gradually increase the website by increasing the number of pages with a couple of clicks, not a couple of weeks work, and adding an additional 50, 100, 250 pages to an existing website and growing it over time.

These pages are designed to rank, and they generate hundreds and, in some cases, thousands of new leads every single month.

So the process is to create one page of content, set a radius around the central location of your business, then let the Magic Page Plugin do the rest.

If a customer takes you on to build pages on their website or wants you to generate more leads to their existing website. Add a Magic Page, set a radius, and let it make pages over time. It is that simple.

Okay. I'll see you in the next chapter.

Software That Can Help

Once you have your pages written and have added them to your website, you wait. This could take several hours, days, or even weeks to get indexed, we have to let it sit and see where it eventually ends up in the Google rankings.

Before doing anything else, we want to let Google pick up the content and figure out exactly how much it likes it. Once the website has been indexed and settled into the rankings, we want to improve the content before doing any off-page SEO.

I have done a lot of work in the mass page industry for many years, and my strategy has always been to build a major city site with several service pages optimizing the homepage to rank in the major city, then create a radius of between 5 and 25 miles around the website by building individual location pages for every single city, town, and village within that radius.

This may sound like long, complicated work, but you can do this very quickly using Magic Page Plugin.

The way the plugin works, you create one page of content that is then used on all of the location pages from the major city right through to the smallest of the village pages. Each page contains the same content but different geolocation data, longitude and latitude data and location information. This works absolutely brilliantly because Google doesn't consider the content on each page duplicate. It is not duplicate content stolen from third party websites, but instead your company message. This is relevant in all your locations, no matter how big a radius your business covers.

What makes the strategy very easy is that we only need to optimize the most challenging location, which in most cases is the major city. Because of the way the software works, we only need to optimize the major city, and Magic Page Plugin will do the rest.

If you create your content using the exact strategy I show above, it will already be much better than the content on 99% of the pages on your competition websites. We let this content bed in and settle into its rankings before we start making on-page SEO changes. This will increase your rankings even further before you ever have to consider off-page SEO.

There is a straightforward way of doing this with a ridiculously cheap tool that works really well from one of the best SEO experts on the planet.

The software was created by a man named Kyle Roof, and it can be found at PageOptimizer.Pro

Before you start running out and purchasing this product, wait. I first recommend extracting the content with PageReWriter, rewriting the content with PageReWriter, adding the content to your website, and wait for Google to index the pages. Next, we see exactly where your web pages sit in the Google rankings before using this very powerful on-page SEO tool. Doing it in stages like this could help you push your web pages up to the top of Google without ever having to build any backlinks.

In 99% of cases, this will be enough to get you a fantastic position on the first page of Google. If the website was just left like this, then your ranking would likely remain long-term. This is because you have such good quality content on the pages of your website and haven't resorted to any shady tricks to get there.

But if you're anything like me, you want the number one spot, and to get the number one spot, you need to start looking at off-page SEO. This is what we're going to cover in the following few chapters.

Remember, all your pages have been optimized to an equal or better level than in the major city. This means the content on them will be far superior to almost all of your competitors' content in the smaller locations.

Single Niche PBNs

PBN stands for "Private Blog Network", and in short, it means a network of websites privately owned. These are regularly used to rank websites through link building in the SEO world, known as backlinks. Still, the draw on the owners of the PBNs to sell backlinks to anyone willing to buy has made the quality of PBNs generally crap as they have become popular. In a lot of cases, they will do more harm than good for your websites.

Another issue you get with PBNs is the links can be removed or devalued at any time. This is because you do not control the PBN and therefore do not control your own business. I have always hated the idea of someone holding the keys to my company's destruction. That's why everything I do is designed to make my network as solid as possible without taking risks that are not completely necessary.

OK, let's get started. So, the first thing you may notice from looking at this chapter is that it's titled "single niche PBNs," not just "PBNs". Now you may have heard of PBNs in the past, but we don't use a typical, standard PBN like you would expect to find another SEO using. We call those general PBNs, and since their use has become famous for SEO, most are very spammy. The ones that are worth buying links in are usually costly.

What is the difference? Well, when a single niche PBN is created, it's not designed just to gain the system. It's actually designed to help your network grow. When done correctly, a single niche PBN will grow your business, generate more leads, and rank your websites. We design our approach to PBNs so even if your top website is taken down by Google, your other websites are constantly pushing up from the bottom, and another one of your websites is waiting to take its place almost immediately.

So how does a single niche PBN work? Well, it's simple. It's a group of websites designed to link to one another to help each other rank for specific keywords.

When building a single niche PBN, we follow specific rules. Firstly, what we do is purchase expired domains or new keyword-rich domain names.

The expired domains will be from the same industry. Suppose you are trying to target, for example, mobile auto mechanics. In that case, you may use a previous dent repair site, Or you might use a previous garage website, or you might use an alloy wheel website. We stay on the general niche and go after domains that have been used in the auto industry before.

Then what we do is we put up our website onto an expired domain, and we leave them alone until they are indexed by Google. Once Google has indexed the websites, we know that Google doesn't dislike the domain, so it will not harm our other websites in our network. I find it hard to leave a website alone once I have built it. However, do this the wrong way and make the website a part of your network too soon. You could potentially add a lousy website to your network of websites and negatively affect them all.

So how do we do it? Well, the answer is simple. We build as many sites as possible on expired and new keywords rich domains, add them all to Cloudflare, activate their SSL, and let them get indexed. Once they are indexed, we use Lead Simplify to track how many leads are coming in on that particular website.

Once a website generates leads, they become the top of our single niche PBN. Our single niche PBNs are not huge. We may have hundreds, if not thousands of websites in our single niche PBN network. However, they are only ever connected by seven to 10 sites maximum.

So, what we end up with is lots and lots and lots of small triangles of websites. You have one website at the top of the triangle with two websites underneath, linking to the top website. You have four websites below the two websites. Each of these sites links to a website above it.

If you want to really go to town on this, you would then have eight websites underneath that, pointing up, and what you'll find is the one at the top of the triangle will be the one that ranks the best.

In the image below, each of the triangles relates to one of your single niche PBN websites. The arrows linking them together represent the links between the websites. As you can see, they pass the links juice up the triangle to the tip. The site at the tip of the triangle will usually rank higher than the other websites in the triangle because it has more votes. The links are like votes in an election, and the more genuine votes your website has from relevant sources, the higher it will rank in Google.

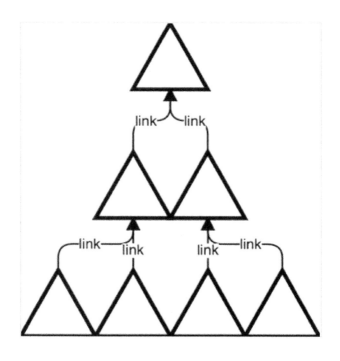

In the image below, you can see multiple single niche PBNs and the structure we use when ranking a website or any other object online. As you can see, each of the single niche PBNs remains entirely separate from one another, meaning they have no connections whatsoever. They are kept like this for safety. Suppose Google decides it doesn't like one of your websites and chooses to deindex it. In that case, it may also negatively affect the rest of the websites in that network. When you structure your PBNs into small triangles like in the image, the worst you can ever lose is one triangle of 7 websites and not your entire PBN network.

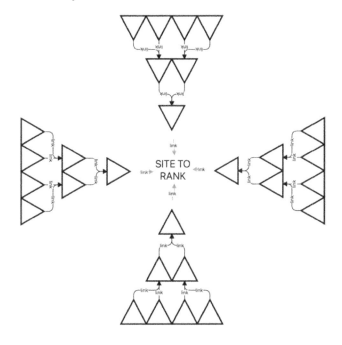

Every website in the network will have a unique form and unique phone number to collect and distribute leads to our lead buyers or website renters. You may have a client renting one website but receiving leads from 5 or ten websites because every single website is designed to help rank the others and generate an income from the leads it produces.

We use the Lead Simplify system to track all the leads to know which websites are producing what leads. We do this because once a website starts to produce leads, we then position that website at the tip of a new triangle to help it rank higher in the search engines organically.

Because we're using expired domains for this, on occasion, you will put up a site and all of a sudden, it starts ranking like crazy in Google. This is awesome when it happens, and the site pays for itself and the network instantly, and you end up generating a lot of leads and can rent the site out very soon.

So let me try to explain how this works. You have a site at the top, you have two underneath that, then you have four underneath that, and maybe eight underneath that, so they form a triangle.

You then have another site at the top of another triangle, another two websites underneath that, another four underneath that and another eight underneath that.

This continues. You could have 5, 10, 15, 20, 30 of these triangles, and what will happen over time is they will help one another rank. Once one of the sites from within the triangle starts to generate a decent number of leads, it moves to the tip of its own triangle. Every site is designed to generate leads. They have a phone number on them. They have a form on them. They collect customer information and pass it to our renters or lead buyers on complete autopilot using Lead Simplify.

You could be passing these calls straight onto a Rank & Rent customer, or you could be passing these calls straight to lead buyers who purchase leads off you.

The more leads a website generates, the more triangles you build underneath it, which we call single niche PBNs, and they help it to rank.

A single niche PBN triangle can be as big or as small as you like. In more challenging niches, the triangles may need to be bigger than the maximum of 15 websites that I use. Just remember, the bigger the triangle, the bigger the loss can be if Google decides it doesn't like one of your websites.

Rather than creating bigger triangles, I create more small triangles underneath the websites I'm trying to rank. This limits the collateral damage if one of my sites happens to be disliked by Google.

Link Building & GMBs (Google My Business)

Link building is not as complicated as it may seem. Citations are just places where your websites have been mentioned. Web 2.0's are generally crappy links, and directory listings are listings on directories.

Another form of links you need to consider are links that you get from paid sources or industry-specific links. These types of links can be pretty powerful if they come from established companies in the industry.

If you decide to become a link vendor and sell links. You can use your single niche PBNs to become a specialist link provider in the niche, or sub-niche your single niche PBNs are created. You can rank other people's websites in the niche with relative ease because you own hundreds of niche-specific relevant websites. These backlinks are potent for the right businesses. Your single niche PBNs are your most powerful ranking tool and the number one business asset for Rank & Rent.

It's also a great idea to reach out to suppliers and other people with similar interests in your business. The same industry, non-compete businesses. Suppose you're in the wedding industry and have a wedding venue. In that case, you may ask photographers, florists, car hire companies, and other such businesses to link back to your wedding venue website. This is considered a backlink to your website from a niche relevant source, which will help your Google rankings.

The best place to start, I believe, is with directory listings. Do a quick search on Google for directory listings. You will find places to list your business in multiple directories simultaneously. I think this is a great place to begin because nearly all industry-specific directories are already indexed. Some of the bigger directories like yell.com provide location-specific listings, meaning you can set up as many free listings as you like. You can also start these immediately. If you're creating multiple listings, then point the links to pages on your website rather than the home page.

You can also use Google free resources like Docs and Sheets to set up mass numbers of links, which may not get indexed but will get crawled, so Google sees them. This has been proved by many SEO tools to provide a minor boost in rankings. However, I believe a more natural linking approach is much better for long term rankings. Therefore, I'm not going to cover spammy linking techniques in this book.

Suppose you are looking to build good quality backlinks to your website. You remain doing only good quality backlinks to your website. In that case, Google has no reason to ever penalize your website for unsavory activity. Because all your websites are designed to rank in the niche and provide a genuine benefit to the searcher. Google will likely never deindex your single niche PBN websites.

I would recommend contacting every business in your industry that is non-compete. Try to work out a deal where you provide cross-promotion, so they link to your website, and you link back to theirs.

Alternatively, reach out to businesses you've dealt with in the past and suppliers, and ask them for a recommendation link to your website. This is long and sometimes dull work, but once it's done, it's done because 99% of these businesses won't review their content for 2, 3, 4, or even 5 years. This means you have a high quality, relevant backlink for that length of time and your website will benefit from that backlink for all that time.

Regarding your off-page SEO strategy, I would recommend getting listed in all the directories and focusing on high-quality backlinks from businesses in your sector.

For each individual website, you should also set up a Facebook page and various other social profiles, where you post regularly. This can be syndicated for free with IFTTT, meaning you do not have to do this manually. You can also get a service from Fiverr called an IFTTT link wheel setup that will automate this process entirely.

Once your websites are rented out. You should speak to the businesses that have rented them and ask if you can get them registered in Google to generate more leads for their business. You then open a new Google account and create a Google My Business (GMB) listing. Then have the postcard sent to the person renting your website home address. which is in the location where you want to receive the leads. Once you have added the code from the card that Google will send out to the website renter, the Google My Business listing will go live. This will generate more leads for the business and is a FREE asset.

On the GMB, you should regularly add images, do posts, ask the renter to send you any special offers they're doing at the current time. Adding these to the GMB often will help it rank in Google.

The best thing about a GMB listing is that it will rank quickly for single keyword searches like locksmith or plumber or pest control in the location where the GMB is listed. Meaning, you get a lot of local searches for single keyword searches that can take six to 12 months to rank for with a local website.

With a GMB, you will rank for these keywords within a matter of weeks and, in some cases, days. You will find that this generates a heck of a lot of leads for the website renter. Be sure to add a number that you control and redirect it to the renter. If the renter ever leaves, you quickly switch off the calls from this GMB and pass them on to a new business.

You should also link out from the GMB to your website, as this will help with ranking the website as a relevant backlink.

If a renter leaves your business and decides they no longer want to pay you every month for the website. You should search for a new renter and instantly follow the same process regarding the GMB for the new business. This will result in you having two Google My Business listings in that location and generate lots and lots of leads for the company.

Once you have several Google My Business listings in a location. You will find that even if the website does not rank, the business receives lots and lots of traffic and lots and lots of customers without you doing much at all.

GMB SEO is quite simple. Add images, add posts, update the information regularly, create a GMB website, and add lots of content to it. There really isn't much else that needs to be done. Most local businesses don't update their GMB regularly, meaning their GMBs are poorly optimized, and yours will easily outrank theirs. You should also try to get the website renter to ask their customers to leave testimonials and reviews on the GMB every time they do a job. This will help your business and help rank your GMB, whether they stay with you as a renter long term or not. This will always generate more work for your clients.

Explain to the person renting the website and GMB from you that they are doing this as part of the team, which is you and them, designed to make their business successful in the local area for a set monthly fee.

So as a quick recap to the chapter. I would recommend getting your website listed in as many local directories as possible. I would also recommend getting your website listed in as many national directories as possible for all the locations you cover. I would set up social profiles for your websites and post to them regularly using IFTTT. I would definitely 100% Get a Google My Business listing for every website you have once that website has been rented to a local business.

If you can't find a local business willing to let you have a GMB registered at their address, do not panic. You can post to websites like Gumtree and Craigslist, offering $50 for somebody to provide a code off the postcards that you post out to that property. You then register a Google My Business listing at their premises. When they give you the code from the postcard, you send them $50. This is actually a brilliant technique. Every time you need to update or re-verify the listing, you pay them an additional $50. It may sound expensive, but believe me, this GMB listing will make you 100 times that amount of money.

Remember, off-page SEO is not something you want to concentrate on early. I would recommend first focus on top-quality content that is well written and long. A few 1000 words of content on every single page, then I recommend optimizing that content, amazingly, using Page Optimizer Pro. Only after you have completed all these steps should you start concentrating heavily on off-page SEO.

Once a website is built and ready, you can instantly start getting it registered and listed in all local and national directories and set up a GMB. But as far as other backlinks are concerned from third-party businesses and things like that, I would not worry about this initially. Once the website is built and starts to rank, focus on relevant backlinks from the industry. This process should remain on the back burner until the website is indexed unless backlinks fall into your lap naturally.

In some industries, it is a lot harder to rank. The content alone will not always provide enough power for you to rank on the first page of Google. This is when your link building strategy will be much more intense. I would recommend joining a community called Internet Marketing Gold. Here you can access all top-level training courses from most of the world's best SEO minds.

This is not something you need to do immediately. Still, it will help your business massively because it is a community full of amazing coaches and SEOs. You're not paying each of them every month for their services. Instead, you get access to them all.

Renting Out Your
Websites

Once your website is built and starting to rank with a steady flow of traffic coming in, you're ready to look at renting out your website.

This is the most daunting part of the process for some people. However, it really is easy. All you need to do is look at businesses with poor quality websites or companies that don't have a website at all.

The aim is to share your new website with them and show all the traffic and leads you're getting that could be theirs for a small monthly fee.

I like to approach this with a try before you buy offer, and I set it up something like this.

Before I ever mention price, the website or anything else. I first like to have a brief chat with the potential client and figure out if they would ever be interested in a website that generates leads in their industry.

After I share the traffic and how many leads my website is getting, and show off with the website rankings. I like to push forward with the strategy that figures out if the potential clients know their numbers and are good potential customers.

The key to renting out a website and making the customer feel like they are getting value for money is to first demonstrate the value of this website to their business. I'll show you how I do this.

I usually ask two straightforward questions before I get round to what price the website will be. I like to look at how many leads the website is getting and use that number when asking my first question. If the website is getting 10 leads a week, I will ask. "If I send you 10 qualified leads a week. How many customers would you get?" If they can answer this question, then I move the conversation onto question two. If they can't, I walk away and find another person to deal with. I will not deal with companies who do not know their numbers because, in general, they are more trouble than they're worth. You don't want to teach your clients to run their business or convert their customers. You just want to send them leads and know they can convert them to customers effectively.

Let's say they get 2 customers for every 10 phone calls coming into their business. That means they have a 20% conversion rate, which is suitable for most Industries and is something we can work on even if it's low.

The second question I ask the customer is. "How much is your average customer worth to you?" For example, if they say $1,000, I know this website does 10 leads a week that this business will be generating $2,000 a week from the website.

I can then close this business and say. "OK, so if this website generates 2 new customers a week for your business and they are worth $1,000 each to you, then this website is worth $8,000 a month to your business. is that correct?"

They must agree because they gave you the numbers. I then say. "So, if I was willing to take $1,000 a month for this website, it would be an absolute bargain for your business.
Do you agree?" At this point, they have to agree, but they really don't want to give you $1,000 for this website today.

Take a breath and let them sweat for a second, and then say. "Don't worry, I won't ask you to pay $1,000 for this website today, but what I will ask you to do is take a 7-day free trial."

"Let's sign all the paperwork today, and if this website does what I say in the next 7-days, you'll have made $2,000, and covered the cost of the website for 2 months. Then just let the payment for the website come out of your bank."

I then continue. "If after 6 days you have had nothing, then just cancel the payment, and we will move on with no harm done."

What you are doing here is you are giving them an easy out and also giving them proof before they ever spend any money with you.

I have on occasion had customers say to me I want to do it but haven't got time. Can we set everything up later? This is them saying no without actually saying no, and my response to this is always the same.

"I've been told by my boss that I must place this website today. Therefore, unfortunately, if you can't run through the paperwork now, I will call (name one of their competitors). If they don't want it, we have a customer who has asked can he sign the paperwork at 4 pm today. Unfortunately, if you haven't got just 2 minutes to make $8,000 this month, then I'm 99% sure the website won't be available in 2 hours."

I know this sounds pushy, and I know you will feel awkward doing this the first time but trust me if there is any chance of signing this client today. They will say yes at this point. If there is no chance whatsoever and they're just desperately trying to get you off the phone, then this won't work, and they may say can I speak to you at another time.

If they ask to rearrange for later. Get an exact date and time, and make sure you call at that exact date and time with an opening line about how lucky they are because the website is still available. But they must grab in now.

Spreading Like a Wave

Before we start this chapter, I will explain what I mean by spreading like a wave. I will then explain why it is such an effective approach when building a Rank & Rent business. In fact, any type of business you want to grow across multiple towns, cities and states.

When setting up your Rank & Rent business. I have already explained that you need to find an industry, choose a sub-niche of that industry, and become a specialist in that specific sub-niche. We start with a single website and rent it out to a company. The company should already be well established in the industry and attend all events, association meetings and other such industry-specific gatherings. If you can rent it out to somebody who runs an association right away, then you have already got a significant foothold in that particular industry.

Once your first website is finished, you then have a process that you can follow for all of your future websites that you know works for the sub-niche you have chosen. When moving onto your next website that you intend to rent out in this sub-niche, you want to stay in the same general location. In the Rank & Rent industry, you will find that most businesses want to rent a website for a major city or a large town local to them.

Let's say you build your first website in the plumbing industry, and that site targets Manchester, UK. You wouldn't build your second website for London as this is over 200 miles away. The chances the first client knows a plumber willing to rent the website in London is very unlikely. However, if instead of going 200 miles away to the biggest city in the UK, you decide to build your next website in Liverpool or Stockport or even Oldham. The chance the person who rents your first website knows somebody in that area to rent the website from you is very high. In some cases, they will even take the second website themselves.

We use this approach when growing our business and spread across the country in the same motion a wave would spread across the country if it broke the shoreline. We utilize the relationships our existing website renters have with all the local businesses. Growing our business becomes much easier. The need to pick up the telephone and cold call pretty much goes away after your first few websites are rented out.

Taking advantage of relationships is probably the best business growth strategy I've ever used. Have you ever been looking for a decent hairdresser, plumber, roofer, electrician, car mechanic? In fact, almost anything we do in life that has to do with repairing our homes, our bodies, or upgrading anything we seek out recommendations.

When a friend has moved house using a specific company and recommends them, do you go anywhere else if the price is right? When a friend recommends a dentist or plumber or recommends somebody to repair or replace anything in your home. If the price is right for you, do you look anywhere else? I'm guessing the answer is likely no. Not only that, but I bet you also feel a strange sense of connection to the person that has been recommended, even though they're just a plumber who has come out to fix your boiler.

It's strange how powerful a recommendation can be, and spreading your business like a wave across the country utilizes those recommendations and results in you having many very loyal clients. Recommendations also mean you don't need to prove yourself every time you pick up a customer because the recommendation already does that for you.

Having an authority in your industry on the payroll getting 10% for every recommendation month-on-month is one of the best investments you will ever make. Not only will they recommend you to every single person they possibly can because they are making money. They will also fight your corner if they hear someone in the industry is not completely happy with your service.

This strategy is very rarely used in the Rank & Rent industry. Still, it's proven to be one of the best client acquisition processes on the planet used by affiliates making millions every month from recommended third-party businesses and products.

I myself have made millions on webinars from my affiliates, and you can learn all about this in my book "How to Create The Perfect Sales Webinar."

So as a quick recap, I would like you to choose an industry then select a sub-niche from that industry that is an inch wide mile deep. Once your website is ready and ranking, you need to rent it out. Preferably to somebody who's already an authority in the industry. Then start spreading your business across the country like a wave. Using recommendations from your existing clients. If you find it difficult to rent out your first website. Donate it to somebody who is an authority in the industry, on the understanding if it generates lots of business, they will recommend you to everybody else in the industry. They still receive a 10% commission on a month-by-month basis from those rentals. Use this strategy, and it is almost impossible to fail when trying to grow your Rank & Rent business in your chosen sub-niche.

If you're thinking, I'm not giving away a website and 10% of my money for an intro. I'll let you try and go it alone for a while first. I guarantee you will eventually come round to my way of thinking. One website and 10% of the profit is a drop in the ocean.

The Website Stacking Strategy

This is something that we could have considered earlier in the book. However, I needed you to understand the process before we start considering the website stacking strategy.

When this strategy is implemented correctly, you can literally double the size of your business without ever finding a new customer to rent your website.

For example, let's say you chose boiler repairs as your original niche. Let's say you are renting out 50 websites and have 150 websites in total. This is because you've also created 100 single niche PBN websites, meaning you have a network of websites that will rank almost any plumbing-related website. You also have 50 paying customers who know your system works and make money renting your boiler repair websites every month.

You are now ready to start stacking your websites and doubling the amount of income you make from every single one of your existing customers. How many of your website renters do you think would do underfloor heating? The answer is nearly every single one of them.

Because of this, we don't need to spread our business further afield. Instead, we target the exact same locations we currently have paying customers, and we follow the exact same process we did for boiler repairs, but this time we are building underfloor heating Websites.

Once the sites are ready and generate many monthly leads, you are literally one phone call away from renting them out.

Call your existing customers and apologize to them. "I'm really sorry I never thought of you for this website before. Do you cover underfloor heating?" The answer will undoubtedly be yes. That is when you can say. "I have this website that has just come free. I was renting it to somebody else for" double what you're going to ask them ", but he has missed a couple of payments, and I've told him he can no longer have the website. We already have an amazing working relationship, and you pay on time every single month. I'm happy to give it to you at 50% cheaper than he was paying, and as we did before, you can start with a seven-day free trial from today. The website will pay for itself before it ever costs you a penny. Sound good?"

This is how you can rapidly grow your business to your same bank of existing customers using the website stacking strategy. All you need to do is find other sub-niches inside the bigger industry and build websites for them.

I would also recommend growing the number of single Niche PBN sites you have as you start to make more money. However, at the outset, the single niche PBN sites you already have will give your new sites a fantastic boost because they're in the same industry and very relevant for your underfloor heating Websites.

This one strategy will literally put your Rank & Rent business on steroids and help it grow exponentially at a rate you never thought possible. Before ever following this strategy, please stick to the beginning steps of the book first and become a specialist in a single sub-niche.

It's Up to You How Far You Take This

About 15 years ago, I was an insurance broker. I had a company car, laptop, phone, a decent salary and beautiful home I could afford the mortgage on easily.

Considering, I didn't finish school, had zero qualifications, and only started my career in the post room 5 years earlier on a £7000 salary, I was doing quite well.

To the outside world, I was a successful career-driven highflyer who had reached the higher end of the income scale in my twenties and had a very bright future ahead of me.

To me, I was trapped in the rat race that society calls life. I felt every single day like the man who owned the company could cut my income with the click of his fingers and destroy my life.

Let's be serious. Most people in the situation I was in live month to month and waste any additional income on a better car, a bigger house and the so-called nicer things in life.

At the time, I was no different from the majority. I was in a job I could see no way out of. I was unhappy and kept making excuses for why I wasn't yet making a move.

I used to sit at my office desk and look around the room at the directors and other senior staff members, wondering what they did when they left the building. I would get in early most days and leave late, as would nearly every other senior member of staff.

The one person I never saw getting in early or leaving late was the guy who owned the company. In fact, he strolled in most days at 11 am and was gone by 3 pm and hardly ever came to work on a Friday. But he still had the best car, the biggest house, the largest salary and the most zeros in his bank account.

WHY?

The answer was simple. He'd made the move to stand on his own two feet and pushed forward hard. His mistakes were his, and he owned them. His successes were his, and he benefited from them exponentially more than any staff member ever could.

He had the balls to make the jump and be the one who carried the responsibility of the whole company on his shoulders.

I was about 28 when the owner decided he was going to sell his company. He secured a deal worth £12,000,000 and made a quick exit to live out his life on a beach somewhere.

As soon as I heard the news, I decided I would make my move, but where would I go, and what would I do? I had no idea. I did know one thing. When I went, I would have to motivate myself to get off my backside every day and push forward because no one else would motivate me.

I realized that the day I walked out on this very lucrative career. I needed to take my choice seriously. I had to pay all my bills and carry the weight of my decision on my own two shoulders.

I knew if I spoke to anyone about my decision, they would try to talk me out of it, so I didn't tell a single person. I also knew there was a good chance I would let them talk me out of it, and I didn't want to end up another overweight 50 something sat at my desk 12 hours a day making somebody else rich.

I closed the lid on my laptop, placed my building pass next to it and walked right out the front door. I had no idea what I was going to do next. In fact, I had no idea how I was going to pay next month's Rent, but I knew I didn't want to become a slave to another man's dream, and it was now or never.

When I walked through the front door of that building, the feeling I felt was excitement and freedom all at the same time. There was also a tremendous amount of fear packed in with those feelings, but I felt great. Instantly, the world felt like a challenge again, like when you first start looking for a job and don't know what your future holds.

I had no prospects, I had no money, I was probably going to lose my home. But I had made the decision that I was never going to pursue another man's dreams for him ever again, and I never have.

Following my departure from this job, I lost everything, including my home. Still, every single day was a challenge for me, and I hit it head-on as hard as I possibly could.

I never looked back, and I have never worked for anyone else since. I went from buying and selling at auctions to spending 12 hours a day on a market stall, to selling flat-pack furniture, to trying to set up a taxi company and everything in between. I must have tried 20 different business models, and every single one of them failed, and each time I had to brush myself off and start over.

Each day was a new challenge, and every failure was mine. I learned from every failure and also every success. No matter how big or small, they were mine, and each new failure took me one step closer to success.

You might look at your life right now and feel like you're in the position I was back then, but you're not. What you have learned in this book has been proven to work thousands of times. Luckily for you, we have a huge community of successful entrepreneurs, including me, who are all happy to help you on your journey.

Before I reveal to you where you can become part of our community 100% free of charge, I first need you to promise me something.

I want you to approach your Rank & Rent career exactly how I approached my career when I walked out of my job and had no plans whatsoever. It wasn't finding Rank & Rent that made me successful. In fact, it wasn't any particular type of work that made me a success. It was my determination to succeed.

Rank & Rent works, and it can work for anyone if you just follow the process and make yourself do at least two hours of work every day on growing your own business.

You are not about to jump into the abyss as I did with no plan or chance of success. If you jump in, do the work and stick with it, you will be successful, and you will make more money than you ever could working for someone else.

Remember:

"Quitters Never Win and Winners Never Quit"

To your success

All the best

Mike Martin
Oops, I nearly forgot, you can come and join me and thousands of other successful entrepreneurs right here completely FREE of charge.

facebook.com/groups/magicpage

Printed in Great Britain
by Amazon

19883095R00058